SNAKES ON THE HUNT

Eye to Eye with Snakes

Lynn M. Stone

The Rourke Book Company, Inc.
Vero Beach, Florida 32964

PHOTO CREDITS
© J.H. Pete Carmichael: title page, p.l4, 16;
© Joe McDonald: p12, 20; © Lynn M. Stone: cover,
p.4, 6, 9, 10, 11, 19

EDITORIAL SERVICES
Penworthy Learning Systems

Library of Congress Cataloging-in-Publication Data

Stone, Lynn M.
    Snakes on the hunt / Lynn M. Stone.
      p. cm. — (Eye to eye with snakes)
    Summary: Describes how various types of snakes hunt, kill, and eat
their prey.
      ISBN 1-55916-263-5
      1. Snakes—Juvenile literature. 2. Predatory animals—Juvenile
literature. [1. Snakes.2 Predatory animals.] I Title.

QL666.06 S87562 2000
597.96'153—dc21   00-025034

1-55916-263-5

Printed in the USA

CONTENTS

SNAKES AS PREDATORS

Snakes are born to hunt. But they don't hunt for sport. Snakes have no choice. Nature made them to kill other animals, their food, or **prey**. Snakes must eat other animals to survive.

Like other animals that hunt for food, snakes are **predators**. Predators are important in nature. Predators help keep the kinds of animals they eat from becoming too plentiful.

Many kinds of snakes eat **rodents**, for example. Without predators, there would be too many rodents, such as rats and mice.

Almost all wild snakes eat living prey. Here a red rat, or corn, snake constricts a mouse.

FINDING PREY

Snakes have special ways to kill and eat their prey. But first a snake must find prey.

Unlike most predators, snakes have poor eyesight. They can see movement over a wide area. But they don't see objects clearly except, perhaps, at close distance.

Snakes don't have sharp hearing, either. But snakes have another way to find prey.

When a snake is hunting, its slender, forked tongue darts in and out. The tongue works with the snake's **Jacobsen's organ** inside the snake's head.

The black-tailed rattlesnake's forked tongue darts in and out to help the snake learn more about the things around it.

7

The snake's nostrils, tongue, and Jacobsen's organ work together to help it smell. Many snakes, then, use smell to find prey.

The **pit vipers** of North and South America can even sense the body heat of their prey. A pit viper, like a rattlesnake, can tell exactly where its prey is. If the prey is moving, the pit viper can tell in what direction, even at night.

A snake may **stalk**, or sneak up on, its prey. Some snakes lie in wait to ambush prey. A snake may also chase its prey.

A southern hog-nosed snake stalks a toad by gliding quietly toward it. In seconds, the toad will be the snake's dinner.

This bull snake is a stranger that no prairie dog wants at the door! These big serpents, looking for prey, invite themselves into prairie dog burrows.

Once coiled, the South American bushmaster can strike out from one-half to two-thirds the length of its body.

PREY

The twig snake of Africa looks like part of the tree on which it hides. The twig snake may use its tongue to lure prey close.

Twig snakes eat small mammals, lizards, snakes, birds, and frogs. These are the kinds of creatures most snakes eat. Some snakes, however, have more special diets.

Some snakes are too small to eat anything except insects. Other snakes eat eggs. The hog-nosed snake of North America lives almost entirely on toads. Another snake lives on snails.

An Arizona mountain kingsnake gulps down a lizard. Most snakes eat a variety of prey animals.

KILLING PREY

Snakes kill prey in one of three ways. Snakes called **constrictors** kill by tightly wrapping the coils, or loops, of their body around prey. A constrictor doesn't crush its prey. The snake's tight coils simply prevent an animal from breathing.

Boas and pythons are the best known big constrictors. Rat snakes are also constrictors.

Certain snakes kill by grabbing prey in their jaws and swallowing it whole. The prey may still be alive as it is being swallowed. Water snakes catch prey, such as fish and frogs, in this way.

The African twig, or bird, snake lies in wait, then stalks prey it sees among the branches. It packs a venomous bite.

15

A third means of killing is **venom**, or poison. Venomous snakes kill by biting prey and forcing venom into the bite wound. Then the venom spreads into flesh and blood.

A garter snake begins to swallow its living prey, a toad, in jaws made to stretch.

KILLING WITH VENOM

Some venomous snakes must bite and hang on to force venom into a bite wound. Cobras, coral snakes, and mambas are among them. Vipers, however, inject venom differently.

A viper has long, hollow front teeth called fangs. The viper makes a stabbing bite into its prey. The viper's venom instantly passes through openings at the fang tips and into the bite wounds. A doctor's needle, filled with medicine, works in much the same way. As it stabs into flesh, the needle carries medicine instantly into the wound.

The Gaboon viper of Africa kills its prey with a venomous bite. This species is the largest of "true" vipers. It can be 18 inches (46 centimeters) around.

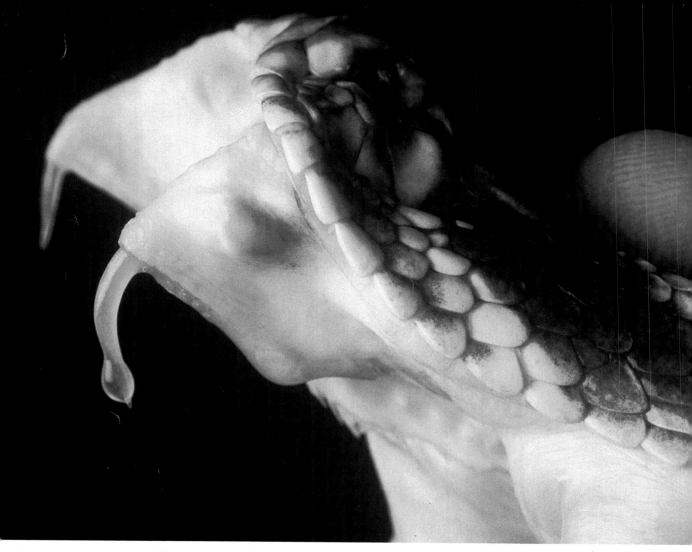

Venom drips from the fang of an eastern diamondback
rattlesnake, one of the pit vipers of North America. Pit
vipers are a group within the larger viper family.

EATING PREY

A snake's jaw bones are connected by skin that stretches. Snakes can stretch their jaws around animals that look much too big to be eaten whole.

A snake, of course, has no manners. It must eat its prey whole. A snake's sharp teeth are not designed for chewing.

Lots of saliva, or spit, helps the snake move the prey from its mouth into its throat and stretchy stomach.

Snakes don't need to eat often. Some species **fast**, or go without eating for weeks or even years.

GLOSSARY

constrictor (kun STRIK ter) – any one of several kinds of snakes which kill prey by squeezing (constricting) it so tightly with their coils that the prey cannot breathe

fast (FAST) – a period of starvation; to go without food

Jacobsen's organ (JAYK ub senz OR gun) – a body part in the heads of snakes which helps them to smell

pit viper (PIT VI per) – any one of several kinds of venomous snakes that have a heat-sensing organ in an opening (pit) in their head

predators (PRED uh terz) – animals that hunt and kill other animals for food

prey (PRAY) – an animal that is hunted for food by another animal

rodent (ROD uhnt) – any one of several mammals, such as rats, mice, and squirrels, that have teeth designed for gnawing

stalk (STAWK) – to move toward prey in a slow and secretive way

venom (VEN um) – the poison produced by certain animals, especially certain snakes

FURTHER READING

Find out more about snakes with these helpful books:

Greer, Dr. Allen. **Reptiles**, Time Life, 1996

McCarthy, Colin. **Reptile**. Alfred Knopf, 1991

Schnieper, Claudia. **Snakes, Silent Hunters**. Carolrhoda, 1995

Simon, Seymor. **Snakes**. Harper Collins, 1994

INDEX

597.96 Stone, Lynn M.
STO   Snakes on the Hunt

Bc 15531

DATE DUE
